FISH & SEAFOOD
◆ ON THE GRILL ◆

Creative Cooking Library

By the Editors of Sunset Books

SUNSET BOOKS
President & Publisher: Susan J. Maruyama
Director, Finance & Business Affairs: Gary Loebner
**Director, Manufacturing
& Sales Service:** Lorinda Reichert
Director, Sales & Marketing: Richard A. Smeby
Editorial Director: Kenneth Winchester
Executive Editor: Bob Doyle

SUNSET PUBLISHING CORPORATION
Chairman: Jim Nelson
President/Chief Executive Officer: Robin Wolaner
Chief Financial Officer: James E. Mitchell
Publisher: Stephen J. Seabolt
Circulation Director: Robert I. Gursha
Editor, Sunset Magazine: William R. Marken
Senior Editor, Food & Entertaining: Jerry Anne Di Vecchio

All the recipes in this book were developed and tested in the Sunset test kitchens. For information about any Sunset Book please call 1-800-634-3095.

The nutritional data provided for each recipe is for a single serving, based on the number of servings and the amount of each ingredient. If a range is given for the number of servings and/or the amount of an ingredient, the analysis is based on the average of the figures given. The nutritional analysis does not include optional ingredients or those for which no specific amount is stated. If an ingredient is listed with a substitution, the data was calculated using the first choice.

Nutritional analysis of recipes: Hill Nutrition Associates, Inc. of Florida.

Sunset Creative Cooking Library
was produced by St. Remy Press

President: Pierre Léveillé
Managing Editor: Carolyn Jackson
Managing Art Director: Diane Denoncourt
Senior Editor: Elizabeth Cameron
Art Director: Chantal Bilodeau
Editorial Assistant: Jennifer Meltzer
Administrator: Natalie Watanabe
Production Manager: Michelle Turbide
System Coordinator: Éric Beaulieu
Proofreader: Veronica Schami
Indexer: Christine Jacobs

The following persons also assisted in the preparation of this book: Philippe Arnoldi, Maryse Doray, Lorraine Doré, Dominique Gagné, Geneviève Monette.

COVER: *Summer Salmon (page 39)*

PHOTOGRAPHY
Victor Budnik: 46; **Robert Chartier:** *6, 7, 9;* **Peter Christiansen:** *3, 32, 34, 40, 60;* **Norman A. Plate:** *16;* **Kevin Sanchez:** *22;* **Michael Skott:** *Cover;* **Weber-Stephen Products Co.:** *5, 7, 9;* **Darrow Watt:** *Inside cover, 4, 10, 30, 44, 56, 62;* **Tom Wyatt:** *12, 48;* **Nikolay Zurek:** *26, 36, 52.*

ILLUSTRATION
Sally Shimizu: *8.*

Special thanks to Weber-Stephen Products Co., Palatine, Ill.

Table of Contents

Barbecuing Basics

Fish and seafood come to market today fresher and in greater variety than ever before.

There are three main types of barbecues —charcoal-fired, gas, and electric—as shown on the opposite page. Your choice will depend on where you'll use your barbecue, the number of people you'll usually be serving, and the kinds of food you're most likely to barbecue.

Charcoal-fired barbecues. The most popular models are open braziers, covered kettles, and boxes with hinged lids.

Open braziers vary from tabletop portables and hibachis to larger models. Many have a cooking grill that can be raised or lowered to adjust the distance between the charcoal and food.

Covered kettles have dampers on the lid and under the firebox to adjust the flow of air and control the heat. They may be used, uncovered or covered, for grilling over direct heat (see page 8). Kettle barbecues are available in various sizes; the 18- to 24-inch-diameter models are the most popular.

Boxes with hinged lids are similar to covered kettles, and can be used covered for cooking by indirect heat, or open or closed for grilling over direct heat.

Gas and electric barbecues. Outdoor units fueled by bottled gas usually roll on wheels; natural gas units are mounted on a fixed pedestal and are connected to a permanent gas line. Electric units are portable; they are plugged into the nearest outlet. All gas units and some electric models use a briquet-shaped material, such as lava rock, above the burner. When meat juices drip on these hot "briquets," smoke rises to penetrate and flavor the food.

Types of Barbecues

Gas barbecue

Charcoal-fired kettle

Portable charcoal-fired kettle

Electric barbecue

Portable gas barbecue

Charcoal, Starters & Fragrant Woods

Charcoal refers to the 2-inch pressed briquets, which may differ somewhat in density and composition. For best results, choose long-burning briquets, and ignite them using one of the following techniques.

Fire chimney. Stack briquets inside the chimney on top of wadded sheets of newspaper, then light. In about 30 minutes, you'll have burning coals ready to use; lift off the chimney and spread the hot coals.

Electric starter. This is one of the easiest and cleanest charcoal starters you can buy. Set the starter on a few briquets and pile more briquets on top; then plug in the starter. After 10 minutes, remove the starter from the pile; in about 20 more minutes, the coals will be ready.

Solid starter. These small, compressed blocks or sticks light easily with a match and continue to burn until the coals are ready for cooking (about 30 minutes).

Propane starter. Simply stack the briquets around the burner; then light the burner and proceed as directed by the manufacturer.

Flavoring foods with the smoke of fragrant woods is an ancient cooking art still in style with modern patio chefs. Several popular fragrant woods are shown below.

Hickory chips

Charcoal

Mesquite chips

Basil wood chips

Barbecuing Tips

When preparing the recipes in this book, keep these tips in mind.

• The recipes were tested with the cooking grill 4 to 6 inches above the coals. If your grill is closer, the cooking time will be shorter.

• Use long-handled cooking tools to avoid burning yourself.

• Wear barbecue mitts for emergency adjustment of the grill and removal of drip pans from the fire bed.

• Use a water-filled spray bottle to extinguish flare-ups.

• Always turn food with long-handled tongs or a spatula—a long fork pierces food and allows juices to escape.

• Salt food *after* cooking (salt draws out juices).

• If using fragrant woods in a gas barbecue, the wood chips usually need to be contained in a pan and used according to the barbecue manufacturer's directions.

• Use small-mesh grills and baskets to keep small pieces of food, such as fish and vegetables from falling through the barbecue grill.

• Be sure that ashes are completely cold (sparks linger for many hours) before you dump ashes into a paper or plastic container.

Propane starter

Electric starter

Solid starter cubes

Chimney

Two Ways to Barbecue

Direct- or indirect-heat cooking techniques differ in how the coals are arranged and in whether the barbecue is covered. For direct-heat grilling, any barbecue is satisfactory; to cook by indirect heat, you'll need a model with a lid.

By direct heat. Open the bottom dampers if your barbecue has them; for a covered barbecue, remove or open lid. Spread briquets on the fire grate in a solid layer that's 1 to 2 inches bigger all around than the grill area required for the food. Then mound the charcoal and ignite it. When the coals reach

Direct heat   Indirect heat

the fire temperature specified in the recipe, spread them out into a single layer again. Set the grill at the recommended height above coals. Grease the grill, then arrange the food on the grill. To maintain an even heat, scatter 10 briquets over the fire bed every 30 minutes.

By indirect heat. Open or remove the lid from a covered barbecue, then open the bottom dampers. Pile about 50 long-burning briquets on the fire grate and ignite them. Let the briquets burn until hot; this usually takes about 30 minutes. Using long-handled tongs, bank about half the briquets on each side of the fire grate; then place a metal drip pan in the center. Set the cooking grill 4 to 6 inches above the drip pan; lightly grease the grill. Set the food on the grill directly above the drip pan. Add 5 or 6 briquets to each side of the fire grate at 30- to 40-minute intervals to keep temperature constant.

Fire Temperature

Use the fire temperature recommended in the recipe.

Hot. You can hold your hand close to the grill for only 2 to 3 seconds. Coals are barely covered with gray ash.

Medium. You can hold your hand at grill level for 4 to 5 seconds. Coals glow red through a layer of gray ash.

Low. You can hold your hand at grill level for at least 6 to 7 seconds. Coals are covered with a thick layer of ash.

Barbecue Accessories

This array of barbecue accessories contains some of the new or updated equipment that outdoor chefs should have on hand. Protect your clothing by wearing an apron. A metal brush does a good job of cleaning the grill if it is still hot.

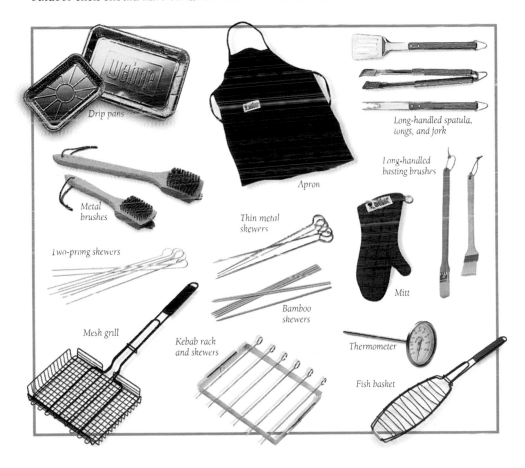

Drip pans

Long-handled spatula, tongs, and fork

Long-handled basting brushes

Apron

Metal brushes

Thin metal skewers

Two-prong skewers

Mitt

Bamboo skewers

Mesh grill

Kebab rack and skewers

Thermometer

Fish basket

Barbecuing Fish

Fish that are both full-flavored and at least moderately oily—such as salmon, trout, halibut, sea bass, swordfish, and tuna—benefit the most from barbecuing, because the smoke enhances their flavor. Smoke overpowers lean, delicately flavored fish.

Shrimp and scallops are easily barbecued when skewered for kebabs. And for delicious appetizers, you can place live oysters, clams, and mussels directly on the hot grill until their shells open.

To help keep fish and shellfish moist while they barbecue, brush them with a basting sauce or with butter or oil. Bastes also add mild flavor. Soaking fish in a marinade before cooking gives it even more flavor; intensity depends on the length of time you let it soak.

Use the direct-heat method (see page 8) to barbecue fish steaks, fillets, small whole fish, kebabs, and certain kinds of shellfish. Use the indirect-heat method (also shown on page 8) to grill whole fillets of large fish, such as salmon, and for chunks and steaks over 1½ inches thick, as well as for large whole fish.

Fillets cook over direct heat; perforated foil supports fish and allows fat to drain off; a baste adds moisture as well as flavor.

For large fish and whole fillets, barbecue by indirect heat. This method allows fish to cook slowly while a foil pan catches drippings.

Special Toppings

Grilled fish may need nothing more to enhance it than a squeeze of lemon. But add a superb hot or cold sauce or a richly flavored butter, and you'll turn even the plainest whole fish, fillet or steak, or shell-fish into a gourmet experience. Marinades, bastes, and butters keep fish moist while they're on the barbecue; toppings add an extra dollop of flavor once they're cooked. Three toppings follow—try them all.

Recipes

Fluffy Lime Butter

¼ cup butter or margarine, at room
*   temperature*
1 Tbsp. lime juice
½ tsp. grated lime zest
Thin lime slices

In a nonreactive bowl, beat butter until creamy; gradually beat in lime juice and zest until mixture is fluffy and well blended. Spoon onto hot barbecued fish, garnish each serving with a lime slice.
Makes about ⅓ cup

Hot & Sour Sauce

¼ cup seasoned rice wine vinegar (or ¼ cup
*   white wine vinegar mixed with 2 to 3 tsp.*
*   sugar and salt to taste)*
¼ cup lime juice
¼ tsp. crushed red pepper flakes

Stir together vinegar, lime juice, and red pepper. Use as a dip for grilled shrimp.
Makes about ½ cup

Fennel-Pernod Butter

⅓ cup butter or margarine, at room
*   temperature*
1½ Tbsp. Pernod or anisette
1 Tbsp. prepared sweet mustard
⅛ tsp. fennel or anise seeds, coarsely crushed

Beat butter until creamy; gradually beat in Pernod until mixture is fluffy. Beat in mustard and fennel seeds.

On plastic wrap, shape butter mixture into a log 1 to 1½ inches in diameter. Wrap snugly; refrigerate or freeze until firm (at least 1 hour). If made ahead, refrigerate for up to 1 week or freeze for up to 1 month.

To serve, slice about ¼ inch thick. Place slices atop hot barbecued seafood.
Makes about ½ cup

WHOLE FISH

To help keep whole fish moist while they grill, brush them with a basting sauce or with butter or oil. Buy your fish absolutely as fresh as possible and have them cleaned, scaled, boned, or butterflied for you at the market. Grill fragile-fleshed fish in a hinged wire fish basket (page 9).

Barbecued Trout

(PICTURED ON PAGE 12)

Before being grilled, these tender trout soak up flavor in an herb-seasoned marinade.

◆

PER SERVING: *279 calories, 17 g protein, .5 g carbohydrates, 23 g total fat, 46 mg cholesterol, 111 mg sodium*

PREPARATION TIME: *30 min.*
MARINATING TIME: *1 hr.*
GRILLING TIME: *12 min. for whole fish; 8 min. for boned fish*

4 *whole trout (about ½ lb. each), cleaned*
⅔ *cup salad oil*
¼ *cup white wine vinegar*
½ *tsp. each dry basil and oregano*
1 *clove garlic, minced or pressed*
¼ *tsp. each salt and pepper*

Rinse fish; pat dry. Leave fish whole, or bone and butterfly.

In a nonreactive shallow pan, stir together oil, vinegar, basil, oregano, garlic, salt, and pepper. Add fish to marinade; turn to coat. Cover and refrigerate for 1 to 2 hours, turning once.

Lift fish from marinade and drain briefly (discard marinade). Barbecue whole fish by indirect heat (see page 8). Cover barbecue and adjust dampers as necessary to maintain an even heat. Place boned fish on a well-greased grill 4 to 6 inches above a solid bed of hot coals.

Cook whole or boned fish, turning once with a wide metal spatula, just until fish flakes when prodded in thickest part (10 to 12 minutes for whole fish; 6 to 8 minutes for boned fish). Using spatula, transfer cooked trout to a warm platter. Accompany with a salsa or mayonnaise.

Makes 4 servings

Barbecued Catfish

*F*ragile-fleshed catfish are easiest to barbecue in a hinged wire basket.

◆

PER SERVING: 341 calories, 21 g protein, 5 g carbohydrates, 26 g total fat, 42 mg cholesterol, 1,401 mg sodium

PREPARATION TIME: *15 min.*
GRILLING TIME: *15 min.*

4 whole catfish (about 13
  oz. each), cleaned, skinned,
  heads removed
2 Tbsp. salad oil
⅓ cup soy sauce
3 Tbsp. each sesame oil
  and minced green onions,
  including tops
1 Tbsp. each vinegar and
  minced fresh ginger
2 tsp. sugar
2 cloves garlic, minced
  or pressed
⅛ tsp. ground red pepper
  (cayenne)

Rinse fish and pat dry. Rub surface of each fish with salad oil, then lay fish on one side of a hinged wire basket with handles. Close basket and secure tightly to hold fish snugly in place; set aside.

In a nonreactive bowl, stir together soy, sesame oil, onions, vinegar, ginger, sugar, garlic, and red pepper. Brush over fish.

Place hinged basket with fish on grill 4 to 6 inches above a solid bed of medium coals. Cook, brushing often with soy mixture, until fish flakes when prodded in thickest part (10 to 15 minutes).

Remove hinged basket from barbecue and open carefully, pulling fish free with a fork if they stick. With a wide metal spatula, transfer fish to a warm platter.

Makes 4 servings

Fish in Leaves

Wrapped in grape leaves, a whole fish retains its juices and flavor.

◆

PER SERVING: 332 calories, 46 g protein, 2 g carbohydrates, 15 g total fat, 126 mg cholesterol, 102 mg sodium

PREPARATION TIME: *20 min.*
GRILLING TIME: *45 min.*

1 whole fish such as salmon,
  red snapper, rockfish, or
  striped bass (6 to 8 lb.),
  cleaned, scaled, head
  removed, if desired
2 lemons, cut into ¼-inch-
  thick slices
2 small onions, cut into
  ¼-inch-thick slices
Salt and pepper
About 24 fresh grape leaves
5 or 6 fresh or dry bay
  leaves

Rinse fish and pat dry. Arrange lemon and onion slices in fish cavity; sprinkle fish with salt and pepper. Grease both sides of a hinged wire basket. Line bottom of basket by overlapping about 12 grape leaves. Place fish on top of grape leaves; top evenly with bay leaves, then cover with remaining grape leaves. Close basket and secure tightly; then sprinkle grape leaves on both sides of basket with water.

Place basket with fish on a lightly greased grill 4 to 6 inches above a solid bed of medium coals. Cook, turning basket every 15 minutes, until fish flakes when prodded in thickest part (about 45 minutes); push grape leaves away with fork to test.

Open basket; peel off and discard grape leaves, bay leaves, and top layer of fish skin. Slide fish onto a warm platter. Cut down through flesh to backbone, slide a wide metal spatula between flesh and ribs, and lift off each serving. Discard lemon and onion slices.

Makes 8 to 10 servings

Barbecued Salmon with Soy Butter

In the Northwest, salmon replaces steak as the most popular choice for the barbecue.

◆

PER SERVING: *417 calories, 38 g protein, 1 g carbohydrates, 27 g total fat, 143 mg cholesterol, 407 mg sodium*

PREPARATION TIME: *10 min.*
GRILLING TIME: *35 min.*

1 *cup butter or margarine*
2 *cloves garlic, minced*
   or pressed
1½ *Tbsp. each soy sauce*
   and dry mustard
⅓ *cup dry sherry or chicken*
   broth
3 *Tbsp. catsup*
1 *whole salmon (6 to 8 lb.),*
   butterflied

In a 1- to 2-quart pan, melt butter or margarine; reserve ¼ cup. Stir in garlic, soy sauce, dry mustard, sherry, and catsup. Keep sauce warm on barbecue.

At the fish market, have your merchant remove salmon head, tail, and back fin, then butterfly salmon from stomach side (do not separate fillets along back) and bone it, leaving skin intact. At home, trim any white membrane from belly area of fish. Rinse fish and pat dry. Lay salmon, skin side down, on heavy foil; cut foil to follow outline of fish.

Place salmon on foil on a grill 4 to 6 inches above a solid bed of hot coals. Brush fish with reserved melted butter, then cover with a sheet of foil to form a small dome.

Cook until fish flakes readily when prodded with a fork in thickest part (about 35 minutes).

Supporting fish with foil, slip onto a large platter. To serve, lift pieces of salmon from foil with wide spatula (skin will stick to foil). Serve with sauce.

Makes 10 to 12 servings

Trout with Carrot Sambal

*A*ccent grilled trout with a tart relish of chile, carrot, and coconut.

◆

PER SERVING: 268 calories, 24 g protein, 17 g total fat, 6 g carbohydrates, 80 mg cholesterol, 132 mg sodium

PREPARATION TIME: *20 min.*
GRILLING TIME: *12 min.*

⅓ cup unsweetened flaked coconut
Water
1 cup shredded carrots
2 to 3 tsp. minced fresh hot chile
2 tsp. minced fresh ginger
½ tsp. each ground coriander and crushed cumin seeds
¼ cup lime juice
Salt
4 trout (½ lb. each), heads removed, if desired
2 Tbsp. butter or margarine, melted
Lime wedges

Place coconut in a small bowl; add hot water to cover. Let stand until coconut is soft (about 10 minutes); drain well. Add carrots, chile, ginger, coriander, cumin seeds, and lime juice. Season to taste with salt.

Rinse trout and pat dry. Sprinkle lightly with salt and brush with butter. Barbecue trout by indirect heat (see page 8). Cover barbecue and adjust dampers as necessary to maintain an even heat. Cook, turning once with a wide metal spatula, just until fish flakes when prodded in thickest part (10 to 12 minutes). Using spatula, transfer cooked trout to a warm platter. Accompany with carrot sambal and lime wedges.

Makes 4 servings

Butterflied Trout with Nut Butter

Easy-to-eat boned trout marinate in an oil-and-vinegar dressing before cooking.

◆

PER SERVING: *545 calories, 25 g protein, 3 g carbohydrates, 49 g total fat, 96 mg cholesterol, 317 mg sodium*

PREPARATION TIME: *20 min.*
MARINATING TIME: *2 hr.*
GRILLING TIME: *8 min.*

4 *whole trout (about ½ lb.*
   each), cleaned, boned,
   fins removed
⅔ *cup salad oil*
¼ *cup white wine vinegar*
½ *tsp. each dry basil and*
   oregano
1 *clove garlic, minced*
   or pressed
¼ *tsp. each salt and pepper*
¼ *cup butter or margarine*
½ *cup chopped salted*
   macadamia nuts or
   hazelnuts (filberts)

Rinse fish and pat dry.

In a nonreactive shallow pan, stir together oil, vinegar, basil, oregano, garlic, salt, and pepper. Add fish to marinade; turn to coat. Cover and refrigerate for 1 to 2 hours, turning once.

Lift fish from marinade and drain briefly (discard marinade). Place on a well-greased grill 4 to 6 inches above a solid bed of hot coals. Cook, turning once, until fish flakes when prodded in thickest part (6 to 8 minutes).

Meanwhile, place butter and macadamia nuts in a small, heavy pan. Stir over medium heat until butter is melted. Keep warm.

With a wide metal spatula, transfer cooked trout to a warm rimmed platter; drizzle each fish with ¼ of the nut butter.

Makes 4 servings

Yucatán Red Snapper

Red snapper, coated in fresh tomato sauce, bakes up beautifully in a covered barbecue.

◆

PER SERVING: *385 calories, 53 g protein, 18 g carbohydrates, 11 g total fat, 92 mg cholesterol, 921 mg sodium*

PREPARATION TIME: *30 min.*
GRILLING TIME: *40 min.*

2 Tbsp. olive oil or salad oil
1 large onion, chopped
2 cloves garlic, minced
4 tsp. sugar
1 tsp. salt
¼ tsp. each ground cinna-
   mon and ground cloves
5 cups peeled, seeded,
   chopped fresh tomatoes
1½ tsp. each lemon juice
   and water
1 Tbsp. cornstarch
1 or 2 fresh or canned
   jalapeño chiles, seeded,
   finely chopped
2 Tbsp. drained capers
1 whole red snapper (5 to
   5½ lb.), cleaned, scaled,
   head removed
⅓ cup thinly sliced pimento-
   stuffed green olives
3 Tbsp. finely chopped
   cilantro

Heat oil in a wide frying pan over medium heat; add onion and garlic. Cook, stirring often, until onion is soft (about 10 minutes). Stir in sugar, salt, cinnamon, cloves, and tomatoes. Increase heat to high and cook, stirring, until mixture is reduced to a thick sauce (about 8 minutes). Blend lemon juice, water, and cornstarch; stir into tomato mixture. Cook until mixture boils and turns clear; remove from heat. Stir in chiles and capers.

Rinse fish and pat dry. Place a 24-inch length of foil crosswise in a large baking pan. Grease foil, then place fish on foil; pour hot sauce over fish.

Barbecue fish by indirect heat (see page 8). Cover barbecue and adjust dampers as necessary to maintain an even heat. Cook until fish flakes when prodded in thickest part (35 to 40 minutes).

Skim watery juices off sauce with a spoon; then stir sauce to blend. Lift foil, fish, and clinging sauce and slide onto a warm platter; drizzle with sauce remaining in pan. Garnish with olives and cilantro.

Makes 4 to 6 servings

FILLETS & STEAKS

*A*ll kinds of fish—from delicate halibut to more assertive tuna—are perfect candidates for the grill. You'll find recipes here for both casual and elegant occasions. Many of the dishes include a marinade, baste, or sauce that adds extra flavor.

PEPPERED SALMON, RECIPE ON PAGE 24

Peppered Salmon

(PICTURED ON PAGE 22)

Inspired by the spicy flavorings of pastrami, peppered salmon takes on a savory quality.

◆

PER SERVING: 153 calories, 18 g protein, 6 g carbohydrates, 6 g total fat, 51 mg cholesterol, 513 mg sodium

PREPARATION TIME: *20 min.*
CHILLING TIME: *4 hr.*
GRILLING TIME: *1½ hr.*

1 cup firmly packed
   brown sugar
6 Tbsp. salt
1 Tbsp. minced fresh ginger
2 or 3 dried bay leaves
1 tsp. crushed whole
   allspice
1 salmon fillet with skin
   (3 to 3½ lb.), cut 1 to
   1½ inches thick
½ cup mixed whole pepper-
   corns (pink, green, white,
   black; for mildest flavor,
   use mainly pink and
   green peppercorns)
½ cup apple or hickory
   wood chips, soaked
   in hot water 15 minutes,
   drained
1 Tbsp. honey
2 or 3 thin red onion slices
Fresh dill sprigs

In a 1- to 1½-quart pan, bring 1½ cups water, sugar, salt, ginger, bay leaves, and allspice to a boil over high heat; stir until sugar dissolves. Let cool slightly.

Rinse salmon, pat dry, and lay flat with skin down in a rimmed 12- by 15-inch pan. Pour sugar-salt mixture over salmon. Cover tightly and refrigerate at least 4 hours. Occasionally spoon brine over the fish.

Meanwhile, pour enough hot water over pepper-corns to float them; soak at least 15 minutes.

Pour brine off fish; rinse fish with cool water and pat dry. Set skin side down on a large sheet of foil; cut foil along outline of fish. Rub honey over top of fish; drain peppercorns and scatter evenly over fish, patting lightly to set them in place.

Place salmon on foil in center of lightly greased grill and cook by indirect heat (see page 8), filling gap between coals with soaked wood chips. Put lid on barbecue and adjust vents to make ¼-inch open-ings. Cook salmon until it is 140°F. in center of thickest part (about 1½ hours). Serve warm, cool, or chilled. Garnish with onion and dill.

Makes 12 to 14 servings

Lingcod with Mint Relish

Subtle seasonings add an unusual dimension to grilled lingcod.

◆

PER SERVING: *163 calories, 27 g protein, 4 g carbohydrates, 4 g total fat, 79 mg cholesterol, 108 mg sodium*

PREPARATION TIME: *15 min.*
GRILLING TIME: *10 min.*

½ *cup fresh mint*
½ *cup cilantro*
3 *Tbsp. lemon juice*
1 *fresh jalapeño chile,*
  stemmed, seeded
1 *clove garlic*
½ *tsp. ground cumin*
½ *cup sweetened shredded*
  dry coconut
2 *lb. boned and skinned*
  lingcod or rockfish fillets,
  each about 1 inch at
  thickest part
Salt

In a blender or food processor, whirl mint, cilantro, lemon juice, 1 tablespoon water, chile, garlic, and cumin until smoothly puréed. Stir in coconut.

Rinse fish, pat dry, and cut into 4 equal pieces. On a grill 4 to 6 inches above a solid bed of hot coals, position fish so grain is at right angles to grill bars. Cook, until edges of fish begin to turn opaque; then, sliding a wide spatula along the grill bars and under the fillets, turn the fish over. Cook until fish is opaque but still moist-looking in thickest part (8 to 10 minutes total); cut to test.

With a spatula, transfer fish to a platter and top each portion equally with the mint-cilantro mixture. Add salt to taste.

Makes 6 servings

Grilled Fish Steaks
with Dill Butter

Seasoned dill butter adds enticing subtlety to grilled fish steaks.

◆

PER SERVING: *377 calories, 34 protein, .86 g carbohydrates, 26 g total fat, 125 mg cholesterol, 195 mg sodium*

PREPARATION TIME: *15 min.*
GRILLING TIME: *10 min.*

¼ cup butter or margarine,
  at room temperature
¼ cup chopped fresh dill
  or 2 Tbsp. dill weed
4 salmon, tuna, swordfish,
  halibut, or sturgeon steaks
  (about 1½ lb. total)
2 Tbsp. olive oil or salad oil
Salt and pepper

In a small bowl, mix butter and dill until well combined. Transfer to small serving crock. Set aside.

Rinse fish and pat dry. Rub with oil. Place on a grill 4 to 6 inches above a solid bed of hot coals. Cook, turning once or twice, until fish is just opaque (or tuna is slightly pink) in center (6 to 10 minutes total); cut to test.

Transfer fish to a warm serving platter and season to taste with salt and pepper. Serve with dill butter.

Makes 2 to 4 servings

Swordfish with Fruit & Citrus Vinegar

The sweet-tart combination of fruit and vinegar adds a tangy accent to fish.

◆

PER SERVING: 271 calories, 36 g protein, 14 g carbohydrates, 8 g total fat, 54 mg cholesterol, 93 mg sodium

PREPARATION TIME: *5 min.*
GRILLING TIME: *10 min.*

4 *swordfish, halibut, or
   sturgeon steaks (1½ lb.
   total), cut 1 inch thick*
1 *Tbsp. salad oil*
1 *cup chopped ripe mango*
1 *cup blackberries, rinsed,
   drained*
2 *Tbsp. chopped cilantro*
1 *cup grapefruit, other
   citrus, or chile vinegar*
Salt and pepper

Rub fish with oil. Place on a greased grill over a solid bed of medium-hot coals. Cook, turning occasionally until fish is no longer translucent in center (about 10 minutes); cut to test.

Place fish on 4 plates. Top with mango, blackberries, cilantro, and ½ the vinegar. Season with salt, pepper, and remaining vinegar to taste.

Makes 4 servings

Sablefish Teriyaki

Spicy soy-sherry baste adds extra flavor to buttery-textured sablefish.

◆

PER SERVING: *407 calories, 26 g protein, 4 g carbohydrates, 29 g total fat, 93 mg cholesterol, 795 mg sodium*

PREPARATION TIME: *15 min.*
MARINATING TIME: *30 min.*
GRILLING TIME: *20 min.*

¼ cup soy sauce
½ cup dry sherry
2 Tbsp. lemon juice
½ tsp. grated fresh ginger
   or ¼ tsp. ground ginger
1 piece sablefish (2 to
   3 lb.) cut lengthwise
   into 2 fillets

In a small pan, combine soy sauce, sherry, lemon juice, and ginger; simmer over low heat for 2 minutes to blend flavors. Set aside.

Rinse fish and pat dry. Place each fillet, skin side down, on a piece of heavy-duty foil; cut foil to follow outlines of fish, leaving a 1- to 2-inch border. Lift fish off foil and pierce each piece of foil in several places with a skewer; set fish back on foil and crimp edges of foil. Brush some of the soy mixture over tops of fish fillets; let stand for 30 to 45 minutes at room temperature.

Barbecue fish by indirect heat (see page 8). Cover barbecue and adjust dampers as necessary to maintain an even heat. Cook, basting fish several times with remaining soy mixture, until fish flakes when prodded in thickest part (15 to 20 minutes).

Makes 6 servings

Grilled Halibut with
Basil-Garlic Butter

Shapely pats of basil-fragrant butter dapple the tops of these hot fish steaks.

◆

PER SERVING: *299 calories, 23 g protein, 122 g carbohydrates, 22 g total fat, 76 mg cholesterol, 215 mg sodium*

PREPARATION TIME: *20 min.*
GRILLING TIME: *10 min*

½ cup minced fresh basil
2 cloves garlic, minced
   or pressed
½ cup (¼ lb.) butter or
   margarine, at room
   temperature
Pepper
6 halibut steaks (1½ to 2 lb.
   total), cut 1 inch thick
2 Tbsp. olive oil

In small bowl of an electric mixer, combine basil, garlic, and butter. Beat until blended. Season to taste with pepper. Use at room temperature; or cover and refrigerate for up to 1 day. If desired, press soft butter mixture into butter molds; refrigerate until firm, then unmold to use. Or spread soft butter mixture into a thin rectangle on a piece of wax paper; refrigerate until firm. Then cut into shapes with a small decorative cutter.

Rinse fish steaks and pat dry; brush both sides of each steak with oil. Place fish on a well-greased grill 4 to 6 inches above a solid bed of hot coals. Cook, turning once with a wide metal spatula, until fish flakes when prodded in thickest part (8 to 10 minutes).

Using spatula, transfer fish to a warm platter. Top each piece of hot fish with equal portions of the basil-garlic butter.

Makes 6 servings

Grilled Chile-Fish Sandwiches

*F*resh chiles, sliced onion, and grilled fish make a richly satisfying sandwich.

◆

PER SERVING: 441 calories, 27 g protein, 38 g carbohydrates, 20 g total fat, 91 mg cholesterol, 172 mg sodium

PREPARATION TIME: *10 min.*
GRILLING TIME: *20 min.*

6 Tbsp. mayonnaise
1½ tsp. grated orange zest
1 Tbsp. orange juice
1 Tbsp. lemon juice
6 sesame hamburger buns,
   split
6 medium-size fresh
   poblano or Anaheim
   chiles (1½ oz. each),
   stemmed, seeded
6 pieces mahi mahi or
   swordfish steaks (1½ to 2
   lb. total), cut 1 inch thick,
   skinned, boned
1 large (½ lb.) mild onion,
   cut crosswise into 6 slices
⅓ cup salad oil

Mix mayonnaise, orange zest, orange juice, and lemon juice. If mixing ahead, refrigerate airtight for up to 3 days.

Brush cut sides of buns, chiles, fish, and onion lightly with oil. Place chiles on a grill 4 to 6 inches above a solid bed of medium-hot coals. Cook, turning often, until skins are blackened (about 10 minutes). Remove from grill. Cool. Remove skin, stems, and seeds.

Place fish and onion on grill; turn often until fish is opaque but still moist-looking in center of thickest part (8 to 10 minutes); cut to test. Split buns and put cut side down on grill until toasted (about 1 minute).

Spread toasted sides of buns with mayonnaise mixture and fill with chiles, fish, and onions.

Makes 6 servings

Charred Salmon with Watercress Mayonnaise

These salmon fillets offer a delicious contrast of blackened skin and moist meat.

◆

PER SERVING: *498 calories, 39 g protein, 4 g carbohydrates, 36 g total fat, 121 mg cholesterol, 225 mg sodium*

PREPARATION TIME: *25 min.*
GRILLING TIME: *7 min.*

1 cup plus 4 sprigs tender
   watercress, rinsed,
   crisped
⅓ cup mayonnaise
2 Tbsp. milk
½ lb. fresh chanterelles
   or oyster mushrooms
1 Tbsp. butter or margarine
4 salmon fillets (6 to 7 oz.
   each), cut 1 to 1½ inches
   thick, with skin on
2 Tbsp. extra-virgin
   olive oil
Lemon wedges (optional)

In a blender or food processor, combine 1 cup watercress, mayonnaise, and milk. Whirl until smooth. If made ahead, cover and refrigerate for up to 1 day.

Rinse chanterelles and drain well. If stems are thicker than ½ inch, cut chanterelles in half lengthwise. In an 8- to 10-inch frying pan, melt butter over medium-high heat. Add chanterelles and stir often until lightly browned (10 to 15 minutes). Remove chanterelles from heat; keep warm.

Brush skin side of salmon with 1 tablespoon oil. Place salmon skin side down, on a well-greased grill 4 inches above a solid bed of very hot coals. Cover grill; cook salmon until skin is charred and crisp and meat is just opaque on top (5 to 7 minutes). Loosen skin from grill with a wide spatula and remove salmon.

Arrange salmon fillets on 4 dinner plates. Divide chanterelles and watercress mayonnaise among plates, spooning the mayonnaise along edge of salmon. Drizzle salmon with remaining oil; garnish with lemon wedges and 4 watercress sprigs.

Makes 4 servings

Grilled Shark Picante

Shark steaks take on bold flavors from a topping of lime-cilantro butter.

◆

PER SERVING: *410 calories, 12 g protein, 3 g carbohydrates, 27 g total fat, 145 mg cholesterol, 501 mg sodium*

PREPARATION TIME: *10 min.*
CHILLING TIME: *30 min.*
GRILLING TIME: *12 min.*

*⅓ cup butter or margarine,
    at room temperature*
½ tsp. grated lime zest
4 Tbsp. lime juice
*1 Tbsp. minced fresh
    cilantro*
*¼ tsp. crushed red pepper
    flakes*
*4 shark steaks (6 to 8 oz.
    each), cut 1 inch thick*
*½ cup prepared mild
    tomato-based salsa*
*2 Tbsp. butter or margarine,
    melted*
Thin lime slices
Cilantro sprigs

To make lime butter, beat ⅓ cup butter, lime zest, 2 tablespoons lime juice, cilantro, and crushed red pepper flakes until fluffy. Set aside.

Rinse fish, pat dry, and place in a 9- by 13 inch baking dish. Drizzle evenly with remaining 2 tablespoons lime juice and salsa. Cover and refrigerate for at least 30 minutes or up to 2 hours, turning once.

Brush fish with plain melted butter. Place on a grill 4 to 6 inches above a solid bed of medium coals. Cook, turning once, until fish is just slightly translucent and moist inside (10 to 12 minutes); cut in thickest part to test.

Transfer fish to a warm platter. Spoon lime butter onto each steak, garnish with lime slices and cilantro sprigs. Offer remaining lime butter to add to taste.

Makes 4 servings

Grilled Fish Steaks with Mustard Sauce

Buttery mustard sauce enhances the delicate flavors of grilled fish.

◆

PER SERVING: *368 calories, 35 g protein, 1 g carbohydrates, 23 g total fat, 101 mg cholesterol, 336 mg sodium*

PREPARATION TIME: *10 min.*
GRILLING TIME: *10 min.*

4 *large firm-textured fish*
    steaks, such as swordfish,
    halibut, sea bass, salmon,
    or sturgeon (1½ to 2 lb.
    total), cut 1 inch thick
1½ *Tbsp. olive oil or*
    salad oil
¼ *cup each dry white wine*
    and whipping cream
1 *Tbsp. Dijon mustard*
2 *Tbsp. firm butter or*
    margarine, cut into
    2 pieces
Salt and pepper

Wipe fish steaks with a damp paper towel; brush both sides of steaks with oil. Place fish steaks on a well-greased grill 4 to 6 inches above a solid bed of hot coals. Cook, turning once with a wide metal spatula, until fish flakes when prodded in thickest part (8 to 10 minutes). Using spatula, transfer fish to a warm platter.

Meanwhile, in a small pan combine wine, cream, and mustard. Bring to a boil over high heat; then boil rapidly until reduced to about ¼ cup. Remove from heat. With a wire whisk or wooden spoon, beat in butter until sauce is smooth and creamy. Season to taste with salt and pepper. Spoon sauce evenly over grilled fish.

Makes 4 servings

Summer Salmon

A basil vinaigrette sets off salmon's distinctive charms.

◆

PER SERVING: *569 calories, 39 g protein, 13 g carbohydrates, 41 g total fat, 101 mg cholesterol, 120 mg sodium*

PREPARATION TIME: *15 min.*
GRILLING TIME: *10 min.*

½ cup each *balsamic vinegar and red wine vinegar*
½ cup *chopped, packed fresh basil*
1 Tbsp. each *minced garlic and fresh tarragon*
2 tsp. *Asian red chile paste with garlic*
½ cup *olive oil*
4 *baby salmon fillets (6 to 7 oz. each)*
8 to 10 cups *(about ½ lb.) salad mix, rinsed, crisped*
2 *large (1¼ lb. total) firm-ripe tomatoes, cored, thickly sliced*

In a blender or food processor, combine balsamic vinegar, red wine vinegar, basil, garlic, tarragon, and red chile paste. With blender or food processor on, slowly add olive oil. Refrigerate until ready to use or up to 2 days.

Rinse fillets, pat dry, and place in a 9- by 13-inch baking dish. Pour ¾ cup of basil vinaigrette over fillets, reserving the remainder. Refrigerate about 1 hour (turn fillets every 15 minutes).

Lift fillets from vinaigrette; drain briefly (discard marinade). Place salmon on a well-greased grill 4 to 6 inches above a solid bed of medium-hot coals. Cook (turning fillets after 4 minutes), until moist-looking but opaque in thickest part (8 to 10 minutes total); cut to test. Remove from grill; cover with foil to keep warm.

Mix greens with reserved vinaigrette; evenly divide among 4 dinner plates. Lay warm fillets over greens; garnish with tomato slices and serve with prepared corn relish.

Makes 4 servings

Grilled Hawaiian Fish in Basil-Coconut Curry Sauce

A coconut curry sauce makes this dish a true island experience.

◆

PER SERVING: 258 calories, 32 g protein, 4 g carbohydrates, 11 g total fat, 60 mg cholesterol, 56 mg sodium

PREPARATION TIME: *20 min.*
GRILLING TIME: *5 min.*

½ cup dry white wine
1½ Tbsp. minced fresh ginger
¼ cup minced fresh lemon-
  grass (tender part only),
  or 2 tsp. grated lemon
  zest
1 Tbsp. crumbled dried
  kaffir lime leaves or
  chopped fresh lemon
  leaves (optional)
2 tsp. prepared Thai
  Muslim curry paste
2 tsp. cornstarch
1 cup canned coconut milk
¼ cup finely shredded basil
6 pieces Hawaiian fish,
  such as ahi, mahi mahi
  or ono (½ to 2 lb.), cut
  ¾ inch thick
1 Tbsp. olive oil
Salt

In a 1½- to 2-quart pan over high heat, bring to a boil white wine, ginger, lemongrass, kaffir lime leaves, and red curry paste. Simmer, covered for 15 minutes.

In a blender, whirl mixture with cornstarch and coconut milk until smooth. Return to pan. Stir sauce over high heat until boiling. If made ahead, refrigerate airtight up to 1 day. Reheat to simmering; if needed, add coconut milk to thin. Stir in basil. Use hot.

To prepare fish, cut off and discard any skin. Rinse fish and pat dry. Rub fish all over with 1 tablespoon olive oil.

Place oiled fish on a greased grill 4 to 6 inches above a solid bed of hot coals. Cook fish, turning once or twice, until done to your liking (5 to 6 minutes); cut to test.

Spoon sauce equally onto 6 warm plates. Set fish in sauce and add salt to taste.

Makes 6 servings

Barbecued Beer-marinated Albacore

A robust beer marinade and a tangy lemon baste add complex taste to fresh albacore.

◆

PER SERVING: 202 calories, 35 g protein, .68 g carbohydrates, 5 g total fat, 78 mg cholesterol, 97 mg sodium

PREPARATION TIME: *5 min.*
MARINATING TIME: *1 hr.*
GRILLING TIME: *15 min.*

1 *boned albacore loin (2 lb.),
   skinned or unskinned;
   or 6 albacore steaks
   (about 2 lb. total), cut
   about 1½ inches thick*
1 *cup beer*
2 *Tbsp. butter or margarine,
   melted*
2 *Tbsp. lemon juice*

Rinse albacore loin and pat dry; then place in a close-fitting bowl or dish. Pour in beer and turn fish to coat evenly. Cover and refrigerate for 1 to 3 hours, turning fish occasionally.

Lift fish from beer and drain briefly (discard beer). Stir together butter and lemon juice; generously brush over all sides of fish. Place fish on a well-greased grill 4 to 6 inches above a solid bed of hot coals. Cook, turning as needed with a wide metal spatula and basting several times with lemon butter, until fish is browned and firm on outside but still moist and translucent ½ inch below the surface (about 15 minutes for loin; 7 minutes for steaks); cut to test.

Makes 6 servings

Swordfish with Tomato-Olive Confetti

This colorful entrée is just right for springtime.

◆

PER SERVING: *322 calories, 29 g protein, 3 g carbohydrates, 21 mg total fat, 54 mg cholesterol, 662 mg sodium*

PREPARATION TIME: *20 min.*
GRILLING TIME: *10 min.*

1 medium-size tomato, chopped
½ cup sliced pimento-stuffed green olives
2 Tbsp. drained capers
3 Tbsp. each sliced green onions (including tops) and lime juice
4 Tbsp. olive oil or salad oil
4 swordfish steaks (1½ lb. total), cut 1 inch thick
3 cups lightly packed watercress sprigs

In a nonreactive bowl, stir together tomato, olives, capers, green onions, lime juice, and 3 tablespoons olive oil until well blended. Set aside.

Rinse fish steaks and pat dry; then brush both sides of each steak with remaining oil. Place fish on a well-greased grill 4 to 6 inches above a solid bed of hot coals. Cook, turning once with a wide metal spatula, until fish flakes when prodded in thickest part (8 to 10 minutes).

Place an equal portion of watercress on each of 4 dinner plates. Set one fish steak on each portion of watercress; top each with an equal amount of tomato-olive mixture.

Makes 4 servings

Swordfish Soaked in Italian Marinade

An oregano marinade adds flavor and moisture to grilled swordfish.

◆

PER SERVING: 311 calories, 40 g protein, 2 g carbohydrates, 15 g total fat, 79 mg cholesterol, 183 mg sodium

PREPARATION TIME: *10 min.*
MARINATING TIME: *15 min.*
GRILLING TIME: *10 min.*

2 *Tbsp. olive oil*
½ *cup white wine vinegar*
1 *clove garlic, minced*
or pressed
¼ *cup chopped parsley*
¼ *tsp. dry oregano*
1½ *to 2½ lb. swordfish*
fillets, chunks, or steaks

In a nonreactive dish, stir together olive oil, vinegar, garlic, parsley, and oregano; reserve ¼ cup. Rinse fish and pat dry. Add fish to remaining mixture and marinate for 15 to 30 minutes, turning several times. Lift out fish; discard marinade.

Place fish on a well-greased grill 4 to 6 inches above a solid bed of hot coats. Cook fish, turning once and brushing often with reserved marinade, until just slightly translucent and moist inside (about 10 minutes); cut thickest part to test. Transfer to a warm platter.

Makes 4 servings

Grilled Tuna Steaks with
Fruit & Teriyaki Sauce

*F*resh tuna should be barbecued just to the rare stage to bring out its succulent flavor.

◆

PER SERVING: 323 calories, 28 g protein, 24 g carbohydrates, 13 g total fat, 44 mg cholesterol, 1,079 mg sodium

PREPARATION TIME: *20 min.*
GRILLING TIME: *4 min.*

¼ cup each sugar and soy
  sauce
6 Tbsp. sake or dry sherry
3 thin slices fresh ginger
4 tuna steaks (1 to 1¼ lb.
  total), cut 1 inch thick
2 Tbsp. salad oil
Salt and pepper
8 to 12 thin slices peeled
  papaya or mango
2 tsp. chopped candied
  or crystallized ginger
1 medium-size green bell
  pepper, seeded, cut
  lengthwise into thin
  slivers

In a 2- to 3-quart pan, combine sugar, soy sauce, sake, and ginger slices. Bring to a boil over high heat; boil, uncovered, until reduced to ⅓ cup. Discard ginger slices; keep sauce warm.

Rinse fish steaks and pat dry; then brush both sides of each steak with oil. Place fish on a well-greased grill 4 to 6 inches above a solid bed of hot coals. Cook, turning once with a wide metal spatula, until outside is firm and opaque but inside is still translucent and moist-looking (about 4 minutes); cut to test. Remove fish from grill and season to taste with salt and pepper.

To serve, place one steak on each individual plate; top each steak with ¼ of the sauce, papaya slices, and crystallized ginger. Arrange ¼ of the bell pepper alongside each steak.

Makes 4 servings

SHELLFISH

Show off with shellfish on
the barbecue. Whether they're
simply grilled in the shell,
then dunked in a tantalizing
sauce before eating, or basted
with a spicy sauce while
cooking, shellfish are easy
work on the grill.

BARBECUED SHELLFISH, RECIPE ON PAGE 50

Barbecued Shellfish

(PICTURED ON PAGE 48)

While shellfish cook on the barcecue, a flavorful garlic butter is prepared alongside.

◆

PER SERVING: 496 calories, 31 g protein, 6 g carbohydrates, 38 g total fat, 266 mg cholesterol, 650 mg sodium

PREPARATION TIME: *5 min.*
GRILLING TIME: *4 min.*

1 cup (½ lb.) butter or margarine
1 Tbsp. lemon juice
2 cloves garlic, minced or pressed
20 to 24 each clams, mussels, and medium-size oysters, scrubbed in fresh water
1 lb. extra-large raw shrimp (about 20 per lb.), shelled, deveined

In a small pan, melt the butter or margarine. Stir in lemon juice and garlic; pour into a small heat-proof container.

Place container of garlic butter on a lightly greased grill 2 to 4 inches above a solid bed of hot coals. Also arrange as many clams, mussels, oysters, and shrimp on grill as will fit. Cook, turning once, until clams and mussels pop wide open (about 3 minutes), oysters open slightly (about 4 minutes), and shrimp turn pink (3 to 4 minutes).

To eat clams, mussels, and oysters, protect your fingers with a napkin and drain shellfish juices into garlic butter. Then pluck out meat with a fork, dip in butter, and eat. To eat shrimp, just dip in garlic butter.

Makes 4 to 6 servings

Grilled Shrimp with Prosciutto & Basil

Wrapped in prosciutto and basil leaves, these shrimp can be eaten hot or cold.

◆

PER SERVING: *290 calories, 39 g protein, 3 g carbohydrates, 13 g total fat, 227 mg cholesterol, 1,100 mg sodium*

PREPARATION TIME: *20 min.*
MARINATING TIME: *15 min.*
GRILLING TIME: *8 min.*

½ cup dry white wine
¼ cup balsamic vinegar
2 Tbsp. extra-virgin olive oil or salad oil
2 cloves garlic, minced or pressed
16 to 20 colossal shrimp (10 to 15 per lb.), shelled except for tails, deveined
8 to 10 thin slices prosciutto (about 7 oz.)
16 to 20 large basil leaves, rinsed, drained

In a nonreactive bowl, mix wine, vinegar, oil, and garlic; reserve 3 tablespoons of the mixture. Add shrimp to bowl and mix; cover and refrigerate at least 15 minutes or up to 4 hours.

Cut prosciutto slices in half lengthwise. Lay 1 basil leaf against a shrimp; spiral meat around shrimp (not tail) and basil. Repeat to wrap all shrimp. Thread a long metal skewer through the middle of 3 or 4 shrimp; run another skewer through shrimp parallel to first (to prevent spinning). Repeat to skewer the remaining shrimp; discard marinade.

Lay shrimp on a barbecue grill over a solid bed of hot coals. Cook just until shrimp are opaque but still moist-looking in thickest part (6 to 8 minutes); cut to test; turn for even browning.

Push shrimp off skewers into a clean bowl; add reserved marinade and stir gently. Serve warm.

Makes 4 servings

Grilled Scallops
in Saffron Cream

*S*kewered scallops are richly gilded with a creamy saffron sauce.

◆

PER SERVING: *311 calories, 27 protein, 6 g carbohydrates, 19 g total fat, 110 mg cholesterol, 183 mg sodium*

PREPARATION TIME: *20 min.*
GRILLING TIME: *8 min.*

1 lb. sea scallops, rinsed,
   drained
⅓ cup each dry white wine
   and chicken broth
2 Tbsp. finely chopped
   shallots
Small pinch ground saffron
   (about ⅓₂ tsp.)
½ cup whipping cream
1 to 2 Tbsp. butter or
   margarine, melted

Pat scallops dry. On 3 or 4 thin skewers, thread scallops through their diameter so they lie flat; set aside.

In a wide frying pan, combine wine, broth, shallots, and saffron. Bring to a boil over high heat; boil, uncovered, until reduced by half. Add cream and return to a boil; if necessary, continue to boil until reduced to 1 cup. (To keep sauce warm for up to 4 hours, pour into top of a double boiler or into a measuring cup; set in water that is just hot to the touch. Stir occasionally, replacing hot water as needed. If sauce is made ahead, cover scallops and refrigerate until ready to cook.)

Brush scallops on both sides with butter. Place on a grill 4 to 6 inches above a solid bed of hot coals. Cook, turning once, until scallops are opaque throughout (5 to 8 minutes); cut to test.

Pour sauce onto a warm platter or 3 or 4 warm dinner plates. Place scallops in sauce.

Makes 3 or 4 servings

Ginger-Chile Basted Crab

A *pungent basting sauce flavors these Dungeness crabs.*

◆

PER SERVING: 201 calories, 24 g protein, 7 g carbohydrates, 8 g total fat, 81 mg cholesterol, 703 mg sodium

PREPARATION TIME: *20 min.*
GRILLING TIME: *12 min.*

¼ cup seasoned rice wine vinegar or ¼ cup white wine vinegar mixed with 2½ tsp. sugar
2 Tbsp. salad oil
1 Tbsp. minced fresh ginger
1 large fresh jalapeño chile, stemmed, seeded, minced
2 cloves garlic, minced or pressed
2 Tbsp. cilantro
1 medium-size ripe tomato, finely chopped
2 live large Dungeness crabs (about 2½ lb. each)

In a nonreactive bowl, combine vinegar, oil, ginger, chili, garlic, cilantro, and tomato; set aside.

In a 10- to 12-quart pan over high heat, bring about 6 quarts water to a rapid boil. Pick up one crab at a time, holding the body from the rear and plunge it headfirst into the water. Cook both crabs at the same time, covered. Return water to a boil, reduce heat, and simmer 5 minutes.

With tongs, lift out crabs. Let stand briefly until cool enough to handle. Pull off and discard triangular belly tab. Lift off shell from rear; rinse and set aside. Pull off and discard red membrane with entrails on body and soft gills. Rinse body well; drain.

Place crab on a greased grill 4 to 6 inches above a solid bed of medium-hot coals. Cook crab, brushing often with sauce and turning frequently, until meat in leg is opaque (10 to 12 minutes); crack open to test.

Transfer crab to a platter. Spoon remaining sauce on crab; top with reserved back shells (optional).

Makes 4 servings

Barbecued Prawns Wrapped in Bacon

Wrap colossal prawns in bacon and thread them onto bamboo skewers.

◆

PER SERVING: *270 calories, 32 protein, 1 g carbohydrates, 14 g total fat, 200 mg cholesterol, 578 mg sodium*

PREPARATION TIME: *30 min.*
GRILLING TIME: *12 min.*

8 *or* 16 *slices bacon*
  (1 *for each prawn*)
8 *extra-colossal raw*
  prawns or shrimp (under
  10 *per lb.) or 16 colossal*
  raw prawns or jumbo
  raw shrimp (10 to 15
  per lb.), shelled except
  for tails, deveined

If using bamboo skewers, soak about 8 skewers in hot water to cover for 30 minutes.

Cook bacon, a portion at a time, in a wide frying pan over medium heat until it is partially cooked but still limp (about 3 minutes). Drain on paper towels.

Wrap each prawn in a slice of bacon. Arrange prawns in pairs on a flat surface, with head ends hooked around one another and tails pointing in opposite directions. On 2 parallel bamboo or metal skewers, thread 1 pair of extra-colossal or 2 pairs of colossal prawns; prawns should lie flat. Repeat with remaining prawns.

Place skewers on a well-greased grill 4 to 6 inches above a solid bed of hot coals. Cook, turning once, until prawns turn pink and bacon is crisp (10 to 12 minutes).

Makes 4 servings

Grilled Scallops with Red Pepper Sauce

Celebrate summer's bounty with tender scallops in a peppery sauce.

◆

PER SERVING: *300 calories, 24 g protein, 5 g carbohydrates, 20 g total fat, 95 mg cholesterol, 506 mg sodium*

PREPARATION TIME: *1 hr.*
GRILLING TIME: *8 min.*

2 small red bell peppers
⅓ cup chicken broth
¼ cup dry white wine
¼ tsp. dry basil
½ cup (¼ lb.) butter or
  margarine
1½ lb. sea scallops (1 to
  1½ inches in diameter),
  rinsed, drained
Melted butter or margarine
  or salad oil

Place peppers in a shallow baking pan. Bake on lowest rack in a 450°F oven, turning often, until skins blister and blacken (about 35 minutes). Cool. Peel and discard skins, stems, and seeds.

In a blender or food processor, whirl peppers, broth, and wine until smooth. Pour mixture into a wide frying pan. Add basil. Bring to a boil over high heat; continue to boil, stirring often, until mixture is reduced to about ¾ cup. Reduce heat to medium. Add the ½ cup butter in one chunk and stir constantly until blended. To keep sauce warm, pour into a measuring cup and set in hot water; stir occasionally, replacing hot water as needed. Do not reheat or sauce will separate.

Rinse scallops, pat dry, and thread onto skewers. Place skewers on a well-greased grill 4 to 6 inches above a solid bed of hot coals. Cook, turning occasionally, basting with butter until scallops look opaque inside (5 to 8 minutes); cut to test. Pour sauce onto plates; place skewers on top.

Makes 4 to 6 servings

Grilled Lobster Aïoli

The fragrance of oranges and tarragon season grilled lobster.

◆

PER SERVING: *408 calories, 21 g protein, 4 g carbohydrates, 34 g total fat, 120 mg cholesterol, 659 mg sodium*

PREPARATION TIME: *30 min.*
MARINATING TIME: *1 hr.*
GRILLING TIME: *10 min.*

½ cup mayonnaise
2 cloves garlic, minced
  or pressed
1¾ tsp. finely shredded
  orange zest
1½ Tbsp. orange juice
1½ tsp. lemon juice
1 Tbsp. minced fresh
  tarragon or ¾ tsp. dried
  tarragon
2 live American lobsters
  (about 2 lb. each)
¼ cup (⅛ lb.) butter or
  margarine, melted
Orange wedges
Fresh tarragon sprigs

In a nonreactive bowl, combine mayonnaise, garlic, ¾ teaspoon orange zest, orange juice, lemon juice, and minced tarragon. Cover and refrigerate aïoli at least 1 hour or up to 2 days.

In a 10- to 12-quart pan over high heat, bring 6 quarts water to a boil. Holding the body of the lobster from the top, plunge it headfirst into the water. Cook both lobsters at the same time, covered. Return water to a boil, reduce heat, and simmer for 5 minutes.

With tongs, lift out lobsters. Cool. Split lobsters lengthwise through back shell. Remove and discard stomach sac, intestinal vein, green tomalley (liver), and any coral-colored roe. Rinse lobster well; drain.

Combine butter with remaining orange zest. Place lobster on a greased grill 4 to 6 inches above a solid bed of medium-hot coals. Cook, basting often with butter mixture and turning occasionally, until meat is opaque throughout (8 to 10 minutes); cut to test.

Transfer lobster to a platter; garnish with orange wedges and tarragon sprigs. Serve with aïoli.

Makes 4 servings

Sage-buttered Lobster Tails

Lobster tails and crookneck squash make an enticing seafood dinner.

◆

PER SERVING: *263 calories, 30 g protein, 6 g carbohydrates, 13 g total fat, 133 mg cholesterol, 658 mg sodium*

PREPARATION TIME: *15 min.*
GRILLING TIME: *8 min.*

4 *spiny lobster tails (8 to
10 oz. each), thawed
if frozen*
4 *medium-size crookneck
squash (about ¾ lb. total),
ends trimmed*
¼ cup (⅛ lb.) butter or
margarine, melted*
1 *tsp. grated lemon zest*
2 *Tbsp. lemon juice*
2 *Tbsp. minced fresh sage
or 1 tsp. dry sage*
Fresh sage sprigs (optional)
Lemon wedges
Salt and pepper

With kitchen scissors, cut off fins and sharp spines along sides of each tail. Set tail, shell side down, on a board; with a heavy knife, split tail in half lengthwise, using a hammer or mallet to force knife through shell. Rinse lobster and pat dry.

Starting ½ inch from the stem end, cut each squash lengthwise 3 or 4 times at ¼-inch intervals, leaving attached at stem end. Fan slices out slightly.

Mix butter, zest, lemon juice, and minced sage; reserve ½ of the butter mixture. Place lobster, shell side down, on a grill 4 to 6 inches above a solid bed of medium-hot coals. Set squash on grill, gently fanning out slices. Brush lobster and squash with remaining butter. Cook squash 3 minutes; gently turn over with a wide spatula, brush with more butter and cook until tender when pierced (3 more minutes). Cook lobster tail 5 minutes, then turn over and cook until opaque in thickest part (2 more minutes); cut to test.

Place lobster and squash on dinner plates, drizzle reserved butter over lobster, and garnish with sage and lemon. Add salt and pepper to taste.

Makes 4 servings

Phuket Grilled Shellfish with Green Chile Sauce

Grill shrimp in the shell, then peel and dip in green chile sauce.

◆

PER SERVING: *159 calories, 24 g protein, 11 g carbohydrates, 2 g total fat, 168 mg cholesterol, 173 mg sodium*

PREPARATION TIME: *15 min.*
GRILLING TIME: *10 min.*

*4 to 6 fresh green jalapeño
  chiles (about 1½ oz.
  each), stemmed, seeded,
  chopped*
*3 large cloves garlic,
  chopped*
½ cup lime juice
*1 to 2 Tbsp. firmly packed
  brown sugar*
*1½ lb. extra-colossal shrimp
  (fewer than 10 per lb.)
  or colossal shrimp (10 to
  15 per lb.) shrimp*

In a blender, coarsely purée chiles, garlic, lime juice, and brown sugar; set aside.

Devein unshelled shrimp by inserting a toothpick through joints in back of shell beneath vein in several places and gently pulling to remove vein. (Or, if desired, shell and devein shrimp.)

Place shrimp on a grill 4 to 6 inches above a solid bed of medium-hot coals and cook until flesh is opaque in thickest part (3 to 5 minutes per side); cut to test. Transfer seafood to a large platter.

To eat, peel off shell and dip shrimp into green chile sauce.

Makes 4 to 6 servings

Grilled Prawns
& Spinach Salad

A sherry-ginger-orange marinade flavors these hefty prawns.

◆

PER SERVING: *267 calories, 24 g protein, 20 g carbohydrates, 9 g total fat, 159 mg cholesterol, 299 mg sodium*

PREPARATION TIME: *25 min.*
MARINATING TIME: *30 min.*
GRILLING TIME: *3 min.*

1 to 1¼ lb. extra-colossal
   prawans (8 to 10 per lb.)
   or colossal prawns (10 to
   15 per lb.)
¼ cup dry sherry
¼ cup rice vinegar or cider
   vinegar
2 Tbsp. Oriental sesame oil
1 Tbsp. minced fresh ginger
2 tsp. sugar
1 tsp. soy sauce
1 tsp. shredded orange zest
3 small oranges
3½ quarts bite-size pieces
   spinach leaves (about
   10 oz.), rinsed, crisped
1 large red bell pepper,
   stemmed, cut into thin
   slivers
Salt and pepper

Peel prawns and devein. To butterfly, cut down back of each prawn almost but not completely through; rinse and pat dry.

In a nonreactive bowl, mix sherry, vinegar, oil, ginger, sugar, soy sauce, and zest. Combine 2 tablespoons of mixture with shrimp; cover and refrigerate at least 30 minutes or up to 1 hour. Reserve remaining mixture.

Cut peel and membrane off oranges. Thinly slice fruit crosswise, then cut slices in half crosswise. In a large bowl, combine oranges, spinach, and bell pepper. Cover and refrigerate up to 1 hour.

Spread shrimp out flat on grill over solid bed of hot coals. Cook, turning once, until opaque in thickest part (about 3 minutes total); cut to test.

Add shrimp and reserved dressing to spinach mixture; mix lightly. Place equal portions on 4 dinner plates. Add salt and pepper to taste.

Makes 4 servings

Index